SIGN LANGUAGE

SIGN LANGUAGE

Adventures in Unfortunate English
from the Readers of *The Telegraph*

Aurum Press

T | TRAVEL
The Telegraph

SIGN LANGUAGE

First published 2014 by
Aurum Press Limited
74–77 White Lion Street
London N1 9PF
www.aurumpress.co.uk

ISBN 978 1 78131 365 7

Compiled by the team at
Telegraph Travel:
Senior Editor: *Oliver Smith*
Contributing Editors: *Natalie Paris,*
Jolyon Attwooll

10 9 8 7 6 5 4 3 2 1
2018 2017 2016 2015 2014

Design: Transmission
www.thisistransmission.com

Printed in China

CONTENTS

Introduction · 006
The Americas · 008
UK & Ireland · 036
The Mediterranean · 064
Africa · 082
Middle East · 102
India · 110
China · 128
South East Asia · 154
Australasia · 182

INTRODUCTION

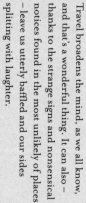

Travel broadens the mind, as we all know, and that's a wonderful thing. It can also – thanks to the strange signs and nonsensical notices found in the most unlikely of places – leave us utterly baffled and our sides splitting with laughter.

That was the spirit in which we launched our Sign Language series back in 2008, in the form of an online gallery boasting a humble half dozen images and a rather tentative call for readers to send in some examples of their own. We were astonished at the response. What began as a trickle of submissions quickly turned into a torrent, and before long we were publishing weekly galleries containing as many as 30 rib-tickling and perplexing photographs, with many more offerings left on the cutting room floor.

Three years later, in 2011, we decided to compile the very best images into the first Sign Language book, and what started as a fun online experiment evolved into a publishing phenomenon. Like *50 Shades of Grey* but with slightly fewer copies (and without the requirement to conceal yours on the morning commute).

And now, though Britney Spears, Woolworths, Lance Armstrong and Justin Bieber have all fallen from grace, we're still going strong, valiantly straddling new media and old. This, our fourth printed book, is a compendium of all the wonderful signs that have made us titter, groan and guffaw during the last year.

We've adapted our format however — because you can't rest on your laurels. While previous editions have seen images divided into themes, this time around we'll be putting the odd in Odyssey, and inviting you on an unforgettable global tour, one which you can enjoy from the comfort of your lavatory seat (or wherever it is you find yourself reading this).

We begin our journey in the Americas, perhaps the best-known continent in the world for its signs, from the garish neon of Nevada to the Tinseltown glamour of the Hollywood welcome sign. Here, the car is king, but best don your corset before you hit the road as some of the signs you see through the windscreen may cause your attention to waver: you'll encounter Fanny Rentals, Whale Washing, and a town called Massacre before the ride is over.

It's a short hop back to Blighty for the next chapter, proving you don't have to travel far to strike Sign Language gold. Just make sure you shut the self-closing gate behind you, as requested.

From there it's over the channel to warmer climes, where the sunny Mediterranean weather seems to have got to the menu printers and sign writers. All aboard the Chaos coach service; first stop Manke Fashion.

Our whistle-stop tour then turns south, through Africa – slowing down, of course, at the spot where dung beetles have right of way – before we make for the Middle East, perhaps giving the Titanic jet ski hire a miss, tempting though that sounds.

There's a brief stop in India, where accommodation at the Kwality Hotel and refreshments from the Wine and Bear Shop are included, before we reach China, surely the spiritual home of bizarre translations. Keep your eyes peeled for the International Ample Bosom Expert and the mysterious 'villain roast bighead', but do not press the Emergency Riot Button.

Our truly global (mis)adventure ends with a dash across South East Asia – where 'foot wearing is prohibited' – before we embark upon the distant shores of Australasia, where we'll hope to avoid spending too long in the company of Dr Snip the vasectomy specialist, or the delightfully monikered Vile & Vile Solicitors.

Send us your signs

As ever, fellow sign-lovers, we'd like to invite you along for the ride, not just for this book but for future editions, by sending your own photographic contributions to signlanguage@telegraph.co.uk and by enjoying our regular online galleries at www.telegraph.co.uk/signlanguage. Bon voyage!

THE AMERICAS

Is anywhere in the world better known for its signs? Think of the giant Hollywood letters announcing your arrival to Tinseltown; the flashing neon of Las Vegas and Times Square, or the familiar signs of Route 66. On this armchair road trip, however, you will glimpse the lesser-seen side of 'Merica and beyond. Not so much big and brash as utterly bonkers.

True to form, we are super-sizing this adventure. Yes, sirree, this ride is going Continental, beyond the borders of good

ol' US of A. In our quest to bring you the region's most outrageous, wacky and memorable linguistic misadventures: a sweeping journey from Alaska to Cape Horn.

Ever the master of the pithy analysis, Oscar Wilde once wrote: 'We have really everything in common with America nowadays, except, of course, language.' Judging from the pages that follow, the words of literature's best-known dandy still ring true.

FEEDING OR HARASSING
ALLIGATORS UNLAWFUL
NO SWIMMING: SURVIVORS
WILL BE TICKETED

→ **VILLAGE IDIOTS**
Location: USA
Spotted by: Casey Musselman

← **ROAD TO RUIN**
Location: USA
Spotted by: Gail Simmons

← **A NOVEL CONCEPT**
Location: USA
Spotted by: Navjot Singh

← **BEST IN SHOW**
Location: Canada
Spotted by: Spencer McKay

→ **PRIVATE HIRE**
Location: Mexico
Spotted by: Lynsey Thorp

↑ **ROAD KILL**
Location: USA
Spotted by: Brian Pierson

← **RECYCLED PETS**
Location: Argentina
Spotted by: Barbara Brown

← FREEZE-Y DOES IT
Location: USA
Spotted by: Rachel Hurley

← CAR PARP
Location: USA
Spotted by: Steven Adams

→ THE WALL OF DEATH
Location: Jamaica
Spotted by: Name Witheld

WARNING

THERE IS NOTHING THAT SEPERATES YOU FROM DEATH EXCEPT THIS WALL. DO NOT SIT ON WALL

→ CRUNCH HOUR
Location: USA
Spotted by: Julian Smith

← FIND ANOTHER SPACE
Location: USA
Spotted by: Mark Spagnolo

← LARGE FLANNEL REQUIRED
Location: Mexico
Spotted by: Bernice Forsyth

← A PLACE TO DIE FOR
Location: Dominica
Spotted by: Mike Farbrother

→ A RUM VOYAGE
Location: USA
Spotted by: Dominic

→ BOTTOMS UP
Location: Canada
Spotted by: Andre Diez De Aux

← PAGAN PARISH
Location: USA
Spotted by: George Adams

← SINKING FEELING
Location: USA
Spotted by: Judy Walton

← THE WHEEL THING
Location: USA
Spotted by: Fred Schimmel

→ WIDE AISLES
Location: Canada
Spotted by: George Massingham

SOD
HOME
DELIVERY

Save $50 per pallet with **FREE** delivery!

-Farm Fresh Sod, Cut Daily
-Multiple Varieties Available
-Discounted Bulk Pricing
-Free Forklift
- 4 Pallet Minimum

Floratam & Bermuda
$159 per pallet

Palmetto & Sapphire
$169 per pallet

Empire Zoysia
$169 per pallet

harmony
TURFGRASS

3 gal
Trinette
$9.98

$16⁹⁸

$16⁹⁸

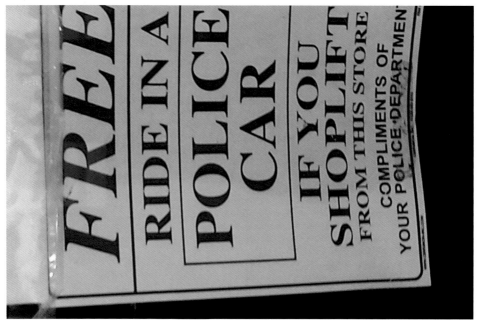

↑ NICKED
Location: USA
Spotted by: David Bailey

← DIRT CHEAP
Location: USA
Spotted by: Tony Rigby

← ELDERLY COUPLE
Location: Brazil
Spotted by: Alan Godfrey

← BATTLE OF WILLS
Location: USA
Spotted by: Nicholas Bratton

→ ROAD TO SALVATION
Location: USA
Spotted by: David Bowen

CHRIST'S HOME
ENTRANCE CLOSED
FOLLOW DETOUR

FIRST PARISH
CONGREGATIONAL UCC

CHURCH
PARKING ONLY
"Sinners will be towed!"

↑ **PERUCULIAR**
Location: Peru
Spotted by: Judith Cronin

← **PARKING POWER ABOVE**
Location: USA
Spotted by: Jonathan Hayes

← TALKING HOT AIR
Location: USA
Spotted by: Sandra Dudley

← SOMEWHERE TO GET PLASTERED
Location: Aruba
Spotted by: Jim McNicol

→ ANY WHICH WAY
Location: Canada
Spotted by: Jane Kershaw

→ **FOR CLEVER DICKS**
Location: USA
Spotted by: Peter Hoyles

← **HERD SHOULDER**
Location: USA
Spotted by: SJ Brooks

UK & IRELAND

Our world tour would not be complete without a rapid dash around domestic shores. For Britain's sign writers are not immune to those grammatical cock-ups and spelling mistakes that afflict their overseas counterparts.

Among this year's submissions was a polite notice at a local leisure centre warning swimmers that – due to a filter malfunction – there was some 'sentiment' settling at the bottom of the pool (how sweet), and a building firm that promises 'quality without compromise'. Our shopkeepers, meanwhile, seem particularly lax at looking after their signs – such as the launderette that it maintains it has 'The Sign of a Good L undr tte'.

But more often than not it was irony, rather than error, that caught the eye of Sign Language contributors while wandering our green and pleasant land. Hence the presence in the following

pages of the Twigg Joinery (surely the last company you'd consider hiring to carry out that attic conversion), a banner boasting of 'indoor seating' at a restaurant called Alfresco, a van emblazoned with 'TDS Electrical Ltd' (be sure to avoid getting lured into a conversation with the dull chap they send to fix the washing machine), and the Maganey Gun Club, which warns of 'Strictly No Shooting' within its grounds.

Either way, it's clear that sign spotters need not be globetrotters – there's more than enough to amuse us on British soil.

CRASH COURSE →
Location: UK
Spotted by: Iolo Davidson

LORRY DRIVERS BEWARE

PLEASE DO NOT DRIVE INTO THIS WALL

→ **HAPPY CAMPERS**
Location: Devon
Spotted by: Geoff Scott

→ **DOWN THE BACK(SIDE) STREETS**
Location: UK
Spotted by: Keith Hughes

← **BLUNDERWEAR**
Location: Cornwall
Spotted by: Ross Hayward

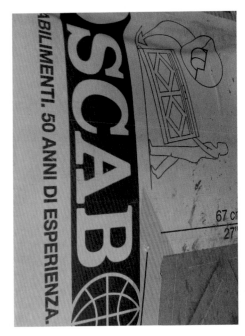

← LEFT IN THE CHURCH
Location: UK
Spotted by: Leonard Stanley

← PICK OF THE BEST
Location: Hampshire
Spotted by: John Reeves

→ CATERS TO EVERYONE'S TASTES
Location: Nottingham
Spotted by: Steve Stone

Indoor Seating at Alfresco

→ **THEY COULD BE HUNGRY**
Location: UK
Spotted by: Richard Beardsall

← **NOAH'S LARK**
Location: London
Spotted by: Brian Minkoff

← ROOM FOR A SMALL ONE?
Location: London
Spotted by: Mark Sharon

← PERFECT FOR WEDDINGS
Location: Essex
Spotted by: Isabel King

→ LOO CONFUSION
Location: Dublin
Spotted by: RF Coyle

SELF
CLOSING
GATE
PLEASE
KEEP SHUT

↑ CAN YOU DIG IT?
Location: London
Spotted by: Chris Wood

↑ SIGN OFF
Location: London
Spotted by: Adam Saul

← CLOSE CALL
Location: Inverness
Spotted by: Dave Drew

↑ A STIFF DRINK?
Location: Wales
Spotted by: Jonathan Scott-Smith

↑ PULLOVER FOR ASSISTANCE
Location: London
Spotted by: Tom Green

→ STOP PULLING MY CHAIN
Location: UK
Spotted by: Phil Male

Please
don't flush

Nappies, sanitary towels, paper towels, gum, old phones, unpaid bills, junk mail, your ex's sweater, hopes, dreams or goldfish

Down this
toilet

人民公社包子　House special baozi　£2.50

面香 Noodles

北京炸酱面		
四川香辣肉丁面 Sichuan Fragrant-and-Hot pork noodles	冬菇拌肉面	£7.80
鸡丝凉面 Cold noodles with chicken slivers		£7.80
炸酱面 Beijing pork noodles		£7.80
四川担担面 Chengdu Dan Dan noodles		£7.80
酸菜鸡丝面 Chicken and picked vegetable noodles		£7.80
西红柿煎蛋面 Fried egg and tomato Noodles		£7.80
清炖牛肉汤面 Aromatic beef broth noodles		£7.80
竹笋牛肉面 Sichuan spicy beef noodles		£7.80
冬菇排骨面 Spare Rib and Winter Mushroom noodles		£7.80
酸菜粉 Sour and hot sweet potato noodles		£7.80

→ **OODLES OF NODDLES**
Location: London
Spotted by: Kate Alley

← **A FREAK OF NATURE**
Location: Chesterfield
Spotted by: Tobias Reynolds

← DRIVEN CRAZY
Location: Lancashire
Spotted by: Charles Fox

← SERVED WITH DRESSING
Location: Oxford
Spotted by: Dennis Stukenbroeker

→ DON'T FENCE ME IN
Location: Norfolk
Spotted by: Chris Allen

Warning

ENVIRONMENT AGENCY

Flood Defence structure.
Please keep clear.

0800 80 70 60

b brickland

Building Developments Ltd

Quality
Without Comprimise

023
8081 4059

34.11

⚡ COCK STOCK
Location: London
Spotted by: Shrijan Sthapit

⚡ SAY IT WITH CONTRACEPTIVES
Location: Yeovil
Spotted by: Stewart Else

⚡ COMPROMISE ON SPELLING
Location: Winchester
Spotted by: Nigel Allan

← YOU'VE JUST GIVEN ME AN IDEA
Location: Norfolk
Spotted by: David Bass

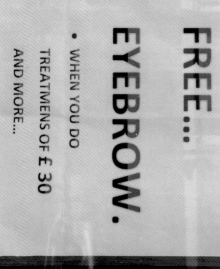

FREE...
EYEBROW.

- WHEN YOU DO
  TREATMENS OF £ 30
  AND MORE...

← YOU COULDN'T MAKE IT UP
Location: London
Spotted by: Mark Sharon

→ GUN MAD
Location: Ireland
Spotted by: Simon Barker

順 Soon Fatt 友
CHINESE TAKE AWAY

→ YOUR NUMBER'S UP
Location: Cornwall
Spotted by: Jo Tully

← ALL YOU CAN EAT
Location: Bray, Ireland
Spotted by: Jennifer Gregan

← STURDY STUFF
Location: Macclesfield
Spotted by: Jacqueline Leonard

← EWE MUST BE JOKING
Location: Sark
Spotted by: Charles Henshaw

→ MAN DOWN
Location: Yorkshire
Spotted by: Dr Rod Edwards

DANGER
Low Flying Humans

DR WHO
FANS
PLEASE ASK FOR
HELP

↑ **SOLD IN PAIRS**
Location: Croydon
Spotted by: Simon Kew

↑ **A PERFECT PAIR**
Location: Edinburgh
Spotted by: Kathryn Medcalf

← **WHO DO YOU THINK YOU'RE TALKING TO?**
Location: Colchester
Spotted by: Kate Garner

THE MEDITERRANEAN

The Mediterranean of the imagination is an idyllic place. Cloudless skies, an infinite coastline and fine sands – it's like all our holiday wishes rolled into one. Artists have been going for donkeys' years. Who knows how many maestros have put brush to canvas with the sun glinting on the azure waters behind their easel? Although one of them, Vincent Van Gogh, did hint at another, wackier side to the Mediterranean when he compared it to a mackerel.

With mass market tourism, the scope for amusing linguistic follies and faux pas has skyrocketed. Words that sound slick

and smart in one language may not quite have the same effect in another. Want to get from A to B? Who wouldn't choose the Chaos coach service? And what could possibly be wrong with the fine restaurant view visible from the 'back side'? Or a boutique advertising 'manke' fashion?

Yes, from mad menu translations to crazy airline names, ever greater links to the Med have opened up a rich, comic seam to our travels. After seeing these signs, you'll agree there's more slapstick in the Mediterranean mix than first meets the eye. Perhaps it's all that sunshine.

REAL TIME →
Location: Turkey
Spotted by: Neil Davies

PLEASE NO PEPPERS IN THE TOILET

→ YOU SNEEZE YOU LOOS
Location: Greece
Spotted by: Hilary Stauffer

↑ BATHED IN SYRUP
Location: Crete
Spotted by: Philip Gibson

← SICK STYLE
Location: Palma de Mallorca
Spotted by: Vivienne Cullingworth

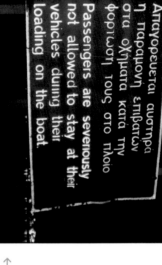

← YOU CANNOT BE SEVERIOUS!
Location: Greece
Spotted by: Joseph Smith

← ORGANISED CHAOS
Location: Spain
Spotted by: Trevor Pogue

→ THE WHOLE TOOTH
Location: Marbella
Spotted by: Colin Jones

JOHN THOMAS

100% FRESH BURGERS AND FRIES

Best in town!

Avda. Just Marlès 25 · Lloret de Mar

→ PRIVATE DINING
Location: Spain
Spotted by: James Heath

← IN THE BAG
Location: Italy
Spotted by: Zena Nattriss

← A CUT ABOVE
Location: Turkey
Spotted by: Trevor Armitage

← LEAKY LOGIC
Location: Italy
Spotted by: Guy Riddell

→ A CRASH COURSE IN LEARNING
Location: Spain
Spotted by: Tom Merchant

Menu

- Souvlaki
- Pork chop
- Lamb chops
- Chicken
- Traditional
- Cretan food
- Omelettes
- Salads
- Breakfast
- Coffee
- Drinks

Terrace with beautiful view at the back side.

Θεα του
ΜΠΑΛΚΟΝΙΟΥ ΜΑΣ

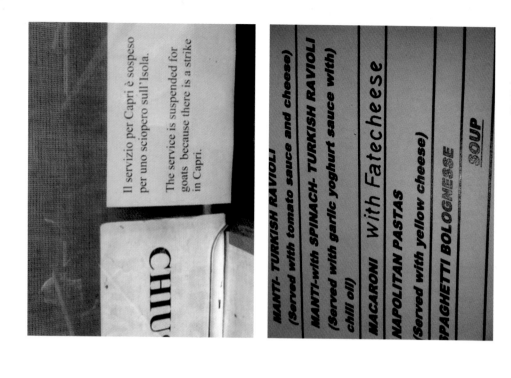

→ WHO ARE THEY KIDDING?

Location: Italy
Spotted by: Paul Jabore

→ YOU KNEW IT WAS COMING

Location: Turkey
Spotted by: Pennie Uygurer

← SEATING IN THE REAR

Location: Crete
Spotted by: Jeremy Leslie-Spinks

Alibaba
Chinese
Restaurant

Excellent, freshly cooked
Traditional chinese food
Reasonable prices
Friendly service
• Take away Available •

Down to the left

← SHANGHAI VIA SYRIA
Location: Portugal
Spotted by: Sean Burns

→ A HOSTILE WELCOME
Location: Turkey
Spotted by: J. Wismark

5- Grilled sardines with fried or wrinkled potatoes (

6- Grilled mackerel with wrinkled potatoes (1) ....

7- Grilled gilthead with wrinkled potatoes (1) ....

8- Griled fFilet fish with wrinkled potatoes (1) ....

9- Tuna fillet with salad and wrinkled potatoes (1)......

10- Tuna fillet in "salmorejo "(sauce made with cand cheese) and wrinkled potatoes (1)........

11- Tuna fillet in dill sauce with garnishing (1)........

BALIK EKMEK

4.50 ₺

FISH IN BRED

↑ **OLD SPUD**
Location: Spain
Spotted by: Rod Edwards

↑ **KIPPER IT IN THE FAMILY**
Location: Turkey
Spotted by: Kevin Crawford

← **FOOT THE BILL**
Location: Greece
Spotted by: James Davies

FISH

13 Fish and you eat friend — 6,50 €
14 Croquettes of cod — • 6,50 €

CHICKEN

15 Filet chicken — 6,00 €
with dads, chips and salads.

16 Nugets of chicken — 5,35 €
with dads, chips and salads.

17 Gordon bleu of chicken 7,50 €
with dads chips and salads.

18 H
19 Fi
wi
20 B
21 S
22 S
w

← GORDON, THE FISHERMAN'S FRIEND
Location: Spain
Spotted by: Martin Fagan

← HOLIDAY BUGBEARS
Location: Turkey
Spotted by: Kevin Crawford

→ HOLLY FOLLY
Location: Crete
Spotted by: Jeremy Leslie-Spinks

Ι.Ν. ΑΓΙΩΝ 5 ΠΑΡΘΕΝΩΝ

CHURCH OF HOLLY 5 VIRGINS

ΝΕΚΡΟΤΑΦΕΙΟ ΑΡΧΑΙΑΣ ΛΑΠΠΑΣ

CEMETERY OF ANCIENT LAPPA

There's a Kenyan proverb that goes 'travelling is learning'. When confronted by strange cultures and baffling languages, the wary visitor needs to think on his or her feet. Especially when confronted with African wildlife. Judging from the following signs, its animals are a constant source of surprise and amusement for our readers. From the penguins that you might find creeping about beneath your car, to randy roadside ostriches, unsuspecting tourists would do well to heed warnings about their more unusual habits. One of the key rules is that – be they large or small – wild animals have right of way. This applies just as much to an elephant blocking your path, as it does to the dung beetles wanting to cross the road.

On such a vast continent, overland travel can take days and you will need reliable directions to get around. Just don't expect a warm welcome crossing the border between Zimbabwe and Zambia.

Helpfully, in touristy parts of Tunisia and Morocco, market stall holders have learnt to overcome potential language barriers by adopting the Del Boy Trotter style of selling. Aside from being immediately transported to Peckham, being reminded of those

bottom-slapping Asda adverts – featuring another British catchphrase favoured by the wily trader – can all but ruin the exotic atmopshere you came away in search of.

Shops can be confusing places also, with bizarrely named products commonly seen on the shelves. Who would want to clean their teeth with something called 'crust'? And what self-respecting housewife would want to buy a soap powder called 'bimbo'? On the other hand, one can assume the stallholder selling chili powder called 'arson fire' knows his target market fairly well. Laugh and the world laughs with you.

CUT ABOVE →
Location: Kenya
Spotted by: Leigh Harries

Dear Customer

All Bags in this Shop are a very
Good Replica of Authentic.
International Brand Names.

The Management

→ AS GOOD AS IT GETS
Location: Egypt
Spotted by: Sergio Cruz

← A GREAT CATCH
Location: Kenya
Spotted by: James Davies

← PRACTICALLY GIVING THEM AWAY
Location: Sudan
Spotted by: Michael Connolly

CHICKEN & CHIPS
FISH & CHIPS
SHISH KABAB / DONATED KABAB / SNACKS

PROIBIDO FAZER
NECESSIDADES AO
AR LIVRE

← NOT ONLY BEARS
Location: Angola
Spotted by: Gavin Cockin

→ MEALS ON WHEELS
Location: Tanzania
Spotted by: Joe Pemberton

→ **MAKING LIFE SIMPLE**
Location: Nigeria
Spotted by: Andy Warren-Rothlin

← **SOUL SEARCHING**
Location: South Africa
Spotted by: Linda Wyness

← BEAK CAREFUL
Location: South Africa
Spotted by: Patricia Taylor

← DON'T CROW ABOUT IT
Location: Africa
Spotted by: Michael Rolfe

→ DUNG ROAMING
Location: South Africa
Spotted by: Nicholas Fry

→ **THE ONLY WAY IS UP**
Location: Egypt
Spotted by: Jennifer Carnegie

← **RELATIVE WARMTH**
Location: South Africa
Spotted by: Mrs Khurram

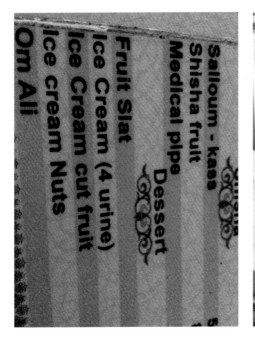

← BRUSH UP YOUR BRANDING
Location: Burundi
Spotted by: Jonathan Wismark

← URINE TROUBLE
Location: Egypt
Spotted by: Michele Groome

→ HOLD IT IN
Location: Egypt
Spotted by: Nicole Cummins

Dear guests,

Kindly be informed that Chill out Bar will be closed today from 18:00 till 19:00.
We do apologize for incontinences.
Thank you for understanding,

Hotel Management

Уважаемые гости,

Мы хотели бы Вас проинформировать, что Chill out Bar не будет работать сегодня с 18:00 до 19:00.
Мы извиняемся за возникшие неудобства и благодарим за понимание

→ HOT FLUSH
Location: South Africa
Spotted by: Jay Dossetter

← A WARM WELCOME
Location: Zimbabwe/Zambia Border
Spotted by: Nicole Beaumont

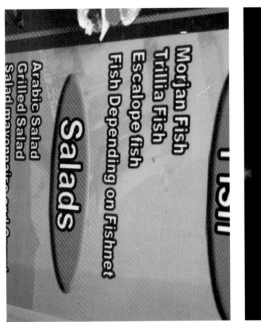

← **TITI WATCH**
Location: Tunisia
Spotted by: J. Wismark

← **WHATEVER'S IN STOCKINGS**
Location: Libya
Spotted by: J. Wismark

→ **THAT'S A RELIEF**
Location: South Africa
Spotted by: Robin Meakings

Sport

Club Med Gym
Every days

- Wake-up Gymnastic :   09.15am
- Abdominal buttocks :   09.45am
- step   10:30am
- Water Aerobics :   11.30am Dou
- body pump   03:00pm at az
- Stretching   04:00pm
                               05.30pm • Rêv

→ RUDE FOOD

Location: Ghana

Spotted by: Mo Ali

← SQUAT AND THRUST

Location: Tunisia

Spotted by: Laurence Harveywood

There's so much history in the Middle East: birthplace of religions and ancient cities. Take Egypt, for example. The writing system of the ancient Egyptians dates back more than 5,000 years. Thanks to the Rosetta Stone (the big black rock, not the CD box set) many of the glyphs were deciphered and discovered to have both semantic and phonetic values. Does any of this help the average traveller tell a shisha from a sheesh kebab today? Only when ascertaining if the glyphs on that souk-bought necklace spell out your name, as claimed.

Despite all this early promise with language, the signs in the following chapter might have you believe that making yourself understood in the Middle East is as difficult as anywhere else in the world.

Menu-wise, it's best to ask for an English translation unless you want to be eating the stringy end of a camel.

A few basic words in Arabic will go a long way, if only to learn that the more persistent calesh drivers are asking for baksheesh (a tip).

So good luck intrepid travellers! If you arrive at Petra hoping to find the Holy Grail, you've been watching too much Indiana Jones. Switch off the television and reach for your Rosetta Stone.

THE MIDDLE EAST

STRAIGHT UP →

Location: Israel

Spotted by: Alasdair Halford-MacLeod

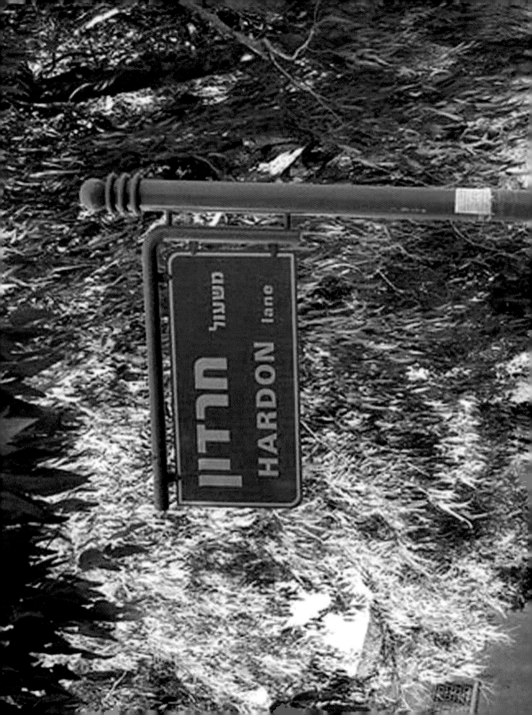

↑ CONSTRUCTION ON THE ROCKS
Location: Bahrain
Spotted by: David Ridgewell

→ I BEG TO DIFFER
Location: Not stated
Spotted by: Michel Mickael

← YOU'VE BEAN HAD
Location: Bethlehem
Spotted by: Howard Marshall

PACKED ON 24-04-2013

MEAT4
THANK YOU!

Lamb Botty

USE BY 27-04-2013

KG/PIECES 0.750

WEIGHT 1

PRICE 0.750

9 945139 007500

← RUMP ANYONE?
Location: Oman
Spotted by: Tim Regan

← BLOW THEM AWAY
Location: Saudi Arabia
Spotted by: Gary Compton

→ SINKING FEELING
Location: UAE
Spotted by: Mike and Alison Thirlwall

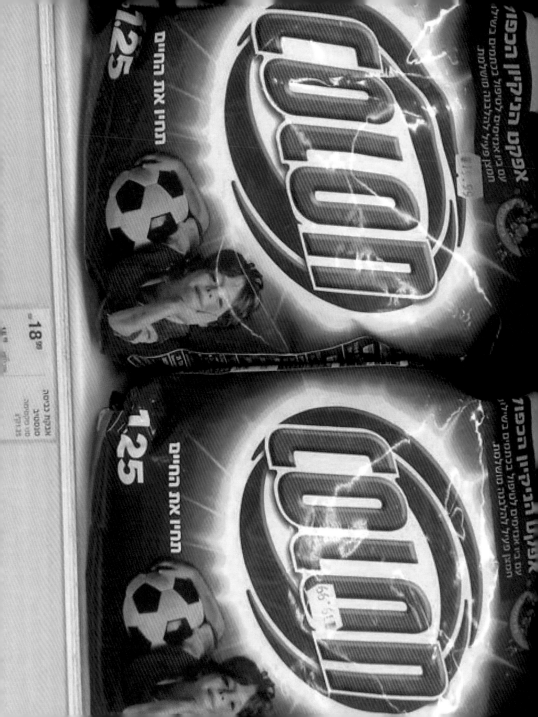

↑ **PAST ITS BEST**
Location: Qatar
Spotted by: Chris Prus

→ **WARNING: HOT**
Location: Oman
Spotted by: Alasdair Halford-MacLeod

← **A LITTLE BEHIND WITH THE LAUNDRY**
Location: Israel
Spotted by: Lydia Rivlin

INDIA

So to India. Final destination on the Hippy Trail. One of the planet's most engaging, colourful, chaotic, spiritual and life-affirming countries. Home to medieval hill forts, sprawling metropolises, stunning beaches and beautiful temples. And – of course – a fair spattering of the world's most confusing signs.

What would all those hippies have made of a van emblazoned with 'for rent dead body freezer box', spotted by one *Telegraph* reader in Chennai? How about a notice advising them to 'use foot over head bridge', seen by another in Darjeeling? Surely a trip to the 'Oil and Dope Store', found in Mumbai, would have been a must for those visitors to India in the Sixties.

Given Britain's close historical ties with the Subcontinent, and our shared love of cricket – a sport where subtlety and attention to detail are paramount – one might expect spelling mistakes and bad grammar to be a rarity when English is required in India. Not so. Among this year's sightings was an advertisement for the 'Gneiss' Book of Records (surely written after one too many pints of the black stuff), a clothing store that stocks an exquisite range of 'jens', and the dubiously-named Kwality Hotel.

Modern day visitors to India – to utilise a cricketing analogy – should expect to find themselves regularly stumped.

WEAR WITH PRIDE →
Location: Chennai
Spotted by: Grahame Gardiner

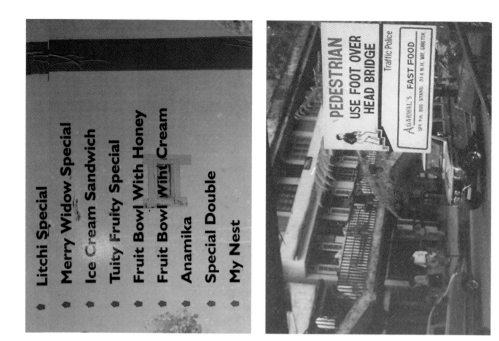

→ **FOND FAREWELL**

Location: India

Spotted by: Hermann Rodrigues

→ **HEAD OVER HEELS**

Location: Darjeeling

Spotted by: Helen Jiggins

← **WOULD YOU ADAM AND EVE IT?**

Location: Shimla

Spotted by: Simon Maddison

← SIGNED, SEALED, DELIVERED
Location: Madhya Pradesh
Spotted by: Shivaram Punathambekar

→ HONEST ALI
Location: Chochi
Spotted by: Rob Parlett

→ CHILLING
Location: Chennai
Spotted by: Grahame Gardiner

17 Lemon Tea / Black Tea / Mint Tea

COLD BEVERAGE'S

18 Diet Coke
19 Coke / Fanta / Mazza / Limca
20 Ginger-Ale/Toxic Water
21 Soda / Mineral Water
22 Lemon Soda
23 Red Bull

LASSI, JUICE & SHAKES

24 Mango Lassi / Strawberry Lassi

→ NAME YOUR POISON
Location: Delhi
Spotted by: Catharine Cellier-Smart

← KWESTIONABLE
Location: Shimla
Spotted by: Linda Cook

← DRIVEN TO DRUGS
Location: Mumbai
Spotted by: Grant Faulks

← GOOD TO GO
Location: India
Spotted by: Susannah Kelly

→ GROG AND GRIZZLIES
Location: Bharatpur
Spotted by: Robert Kaye

WINE ᴬᴺᴰ BEAR SHOP NAGLA UNCH

अंग्रेजी व देशी शराब की दुकान नागला ऊंचा (म...

ठंडी बी...

अंग्रेजी शराब

कल्याण भवन

↱ RE-THINK REQUIRED
Location: Delhi
Spotted by: Catharine Cellier-Smart

↱ WHAT'S IN A NAME?
Location: Cochin
Spotted by: David Clinker

↰ BEARDY WEIRDY
Location: Jaisalmer
Spotted by: David Drew

BUY

ANGOSTURA WHITE RUM 100CL

GET

LITTLE CRICKET BAT & BALL

AUTOGRAPH BY

MR.BRAIN LARA

← HEAD ON DOWN
Location: India
Spotted by: Alison Wright

→ KEEP IT SIMPLE
Location: Kovalam
Spotted by: David Drew

ਬੱਚਾ ਸੀਟ ਪਰ ਬੈਠ ਹੋ ਤੋ

ਫਲੱਸ਼ ਨ ਚਲਾਓ

DO NOT OPERATE FLUSH
WHILE CHILD IS SEATED

D282-77008_521

→ ITCH TO THEIR OWN

Location: Agra

Spotted by: Annabel Sykes

→ WAY TO SPEND A SUMMER

Location: India

Spotted by: Name withheld

← BYE BYE BABY

Location: Air India flight

Spotted by: Dr Roger Litton

← FANCY PANTS
Location: Maner
Spotted by: Tony Kemp-Jones

→ COMPLIMENTARY ODORS
Location: Mumbai
Spotted by: Keith Lanan

CHINA

There can be few more challenging destinations to explore than China. It's geographically vast, its language and alphabet an utter mystery, and – if Wikipedia is to be trusted – just 0.77 per cent of its 1.3 billion population speak English. Need directions to your hotel? You'll need to ask, on average, 130 people, until those puzzled faces are replaced by a knowing nod. Either that, or figure out how to say 'Four Seasons' using only hand gestures.

For people that do make the trip, therefore, reliance on English translations is huge. Unfortunately, those tasked with posting helpful notices at tourist attractions, airports and hotels, haven't done an awfully good job – China is famous for its bizarre mistranslations. 'Chinglish', as such examples are commonly known, is so widespread that the Chinese government has launched successive campaigns – ahead of the 2008 Beijing Olympics and the 2010 Shanghai Expo – aimed at eradicating them. What would overseas visitors think, it wondered, of such ham-fisted attempts to communicate with the English-speaking world?

If the following gems are anything to go by, the grammatical crusade was an utter failure.

Oddities spotted by *Telegraph* Travel readers in the People's Republic this year included an advertisement for an 'ample bosom expert', menus offering 'miscellaneous bacterium' and 'villain roast bighead', and – most puzzling of all – a notice proclaiming 'the cedar group dancing waterfall to fly in the mandarin duck pond the myth biography'. Quite.

THE WORLD'S BREAST JOB →
Location: Suzhou
Spotted by: Anthony Steward

請勿上下車

Do Not Get On or Off

→ **BRITAIN ÜBER ALLES**
Location: Beijing
Spotted by: Jonathan Watkins

← **METRO MADNESS**
Location: Shenzhen
Spotted by: Barclay Bram-Shoemaker

[粥教社]
The village of gruel
GuangZhou · China

← GOODBYE GRUEL WORLD
Location: Guangzhou
Spotted by: Mark Sharon

古杉群舞瀑布飞
鸳鸯池中神话传
The cedar group dancing waterfall to fly
in the mandarin duck pond the myth
biography

← MALLARD TO UNDERSTAND
Location: Sichuan
Spotted by: Phil Tizzard

→ QUACKERS
Location: China
Spotted by: Kim Parker

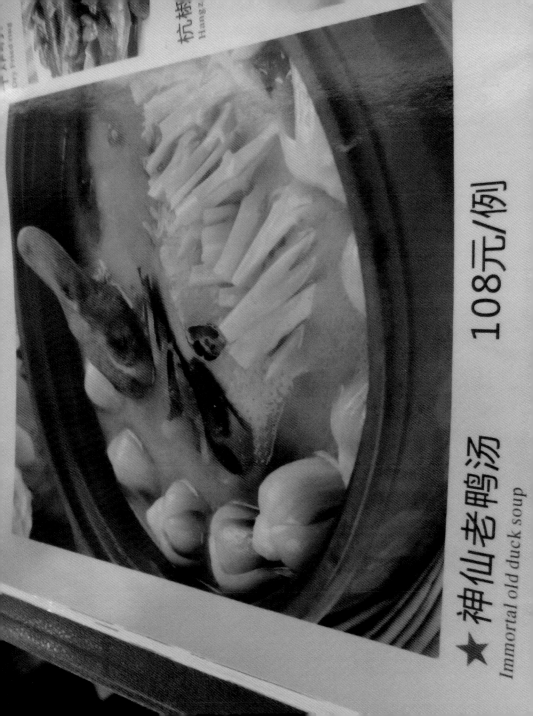

★ 神仙老鸭汤　108元/例

Immortal old duck soup

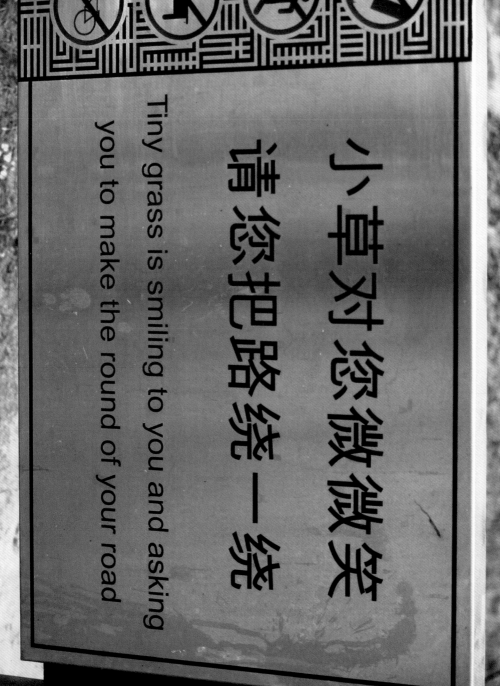

小草对您微微笑
请您把路绕一绕

Tiny grass is smiling to you and asking
you to make the round of your road

→ NEIGH GOOD
Location: China
Spotted by: Patricia Wright

← SPROUTING NONSENSE
Location: Xi'an
Spotted by: Katrin Winter

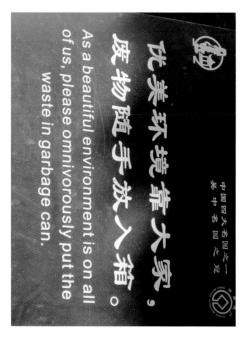

不要將垃圾廢物放入廁所
請自行帶走處理
以免塞渠

Note

Do not waste the waste into the toilet
To avoid drainage plug
Take away your own deal

Catatan

Jangan buang sampah ke toilet
Untuk menghindari konektor drainase
Mengambil kesepakatan sendiri

← RAW DEAL
Location: Hangzhou
Spotted by: Jason Harris

优美环境靠大家，
废物随手放入箱。

As a beautiful environment is on all
of us, please omnivorously put the
waste in garbage can.

中国四大名园之一
美中吾园之冠

← TALKING RUBBISH
Location: China
Spotted by: Elaine Bailey

→ RUNNING MAD
Location: Tiger Leaping Gorge
Spotted by: Karen Hamilton

此段200米，当心落石，请靠岩壁行走，快速通过请勿逗留．

Within 200 meters,notice the rockslide,please is run about by cliff.

车打芝士腌肉蘑菇面

The car hit cheese bacon mushroom face

￥2

渣辣椒炒脆臊 36.00 元/份
32.00 元/份(会员价)
Slag peppers fried crisp smell of urine

渣辣椒炒鸡蛋 32.00 元/份
Konjak with spicy sauce

→ THE KONJAK IS VERY POPULAR...
Location: Beijing
Spotted by: Albert Brown

← WHO ARE YOU CALLING MUSHROOM FACE?
Location: Wuhan
Spotted by: William Gillin

← EASY UNDER
Location: Yunnan
Spotted by: Ali MacKenzie

← A WRITE-OFF
Location: China
Spotted by: David Orr

→ WHERE THE CUSTOMER IS NEVER RIGHT
Location: Yungshuo
Spotted by: Bobby Duncan

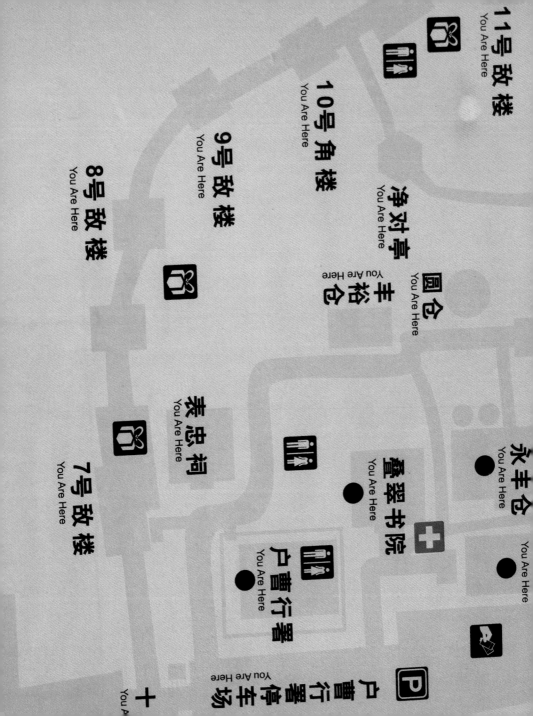

11号敌楼
You Are Here

10号角楼
You Are Here

9号敌楼
You Are Here

8号敌楼
You Are Here

净对亭
You Are Here

丰裕仓
You Are Here

圆仓
You Are Here

表忠祠
You Are Here

7号敌楼
You Are Here

荟翠书院
You Are Here

户曹行署
You Are Here

永丰仓
You Are Here

You Are Here

户曹行署停车场
You Are Here

→ TIGHT SQUEEZE
Location: Shenzhen
Spotted by: Barclay Bram-Shoemaker

← ALL OVER THE PLACE
Location: Great Wall of China
Spotted by: Dennis Tricker

← HEAD CASE
Location: China
Spotted by: P. Thomas

← PEE FREELY
Location: Hunan
Spotted by: Federico Abbasciano

→ NOT NECESSARILY IN THAT ORDER
Location: Jingzhou
Spotted by: John Hotchkiss

为了您的家庭幸福
请远离黄、赌、毒

for your family happiness, please keep yellow. gambling. poison

玉丰国际大酒店

村夫烤胖头鱼

Villain roast bighead

RMB:68元/例

→ GETTING PUSHY
Location: Suzhou
Spotted by: Anthony Steward

← DASTARDLY DISH
Location: China
Spotted by: Bill Dixon

请勿拍打

NO BEATING

YU KEE FOOD CO.,L...

← **HITTING OUT**
Location: China
Spotted by: Vanessa Wei

← **DODGY DINING**
Location: Hong Kong
Spotted by: Sam Baird

→ **I'LL PASS, THANKS**
Location: Beijing
Spotted by: Rachael McGuinness

Brothers

1pic ￥8元

品名：芝士核桃

产地：北京 等级：合格 价格：8元 规格：／ 单位：个 物价员：01

北京市发展和改革委员会监制 Z01－111

【特定原材料】

奶酪 & 核桃

Cheese & Semen juglandis

麦兄弟の面包工房

老人、儿童上扶梯时需有家人陪同

When old man's child go up hand ladder temporary need the family to accompany

请勿踩踏
Do not stampede

→ **RUN RIOT**
Location: China
Spotted by: Name withheld

← **OUT OF STEP**
Location: Hangzhou
Spotted by: Jason Harris

咖喱杂菌煲

Miscellaneous bacterium clay pot curry

RMB:28元/例

← IS THAT THE HEALTHY BACTERIUM?
Location: China
Spotted by: Bill Dixon

→ THE GRASSED LAUGH
Location: Hangzhou
Spotted by: James Hardy

RAMADA PLAZA
HANGZHOU RIVERSIDE
杭州华美达酒店

爱护绿地，请脚下留情！
Prevent the cruelty of green, please show leniency, Do not step on the grass!

铁丝涂有防锈油，小心衣物！
The iron wire wears the anticorrosive oil, Please pay attention to your cloth!

杭州华美达酒店
Ramada Plaza Hangzhou

SOUTH EAST ASIA

The written language of countries in South East Asia, to an ignorant foreigner, appears as an incomprehensible muddle of squiggles and loops, with a few semi-quavers thrown in for good measure. Which is why, in Thailand, most restaurants will pre-empt your need for menus in English. That way it is easier to distinguish between the doodles describing each course and the noodles you want to see arrive on your plate.

These English translations may not be wholly reliable however. As the next few pages show, some of the best 'Engrish' is unintentionally hilarious.

Other phrases, in actual English, are seen with such regularity on Asia's backpacking trail that they become part of acceptable usage – whether they make sense or not. The popularity of the phrase, 'why not?' in South East Asian countries – as a noncommittal response to any awkward question you might have – has spawned at least one bar of the same name in every tourist town.

'Same, same but different' is another overused phrase. Generally (we think) it means that, even though what you have asked for is not available, the person you are talking to knows someone, somewhere, who can get something for you that may or may not be anything like it. You might not completely understand each other but you will reach a kind of agreement, so in many ways, the system works.

And, as any traveller who has been to Laos will verify, what does it matter if bad translations mean it takes longer to work out a minivan's destination? Yours is unlikely to be leaving for a good few hours anyway.

FOOD FOR THOUGHT →
Location: Indonesia
Spotted by: Chris Reece

Roti'O

flavor hard to describe ∘∘∘

↑ LEGLESS
Location: Burma
Spotted by: David Drew

↑ OFF THE RAILS
Location: Jakarta
Spotted by: Paul Bruthiaux

← TWO SCOOPS
Location: Indonesia
Spotted by: Chris Reece

← MY NINE FRIENDS AND I WERE OFFENDED
Location: Jakarta
Spotted by: Stephen Wagstaff

← WINGING IT
Location: Kuala Lumpur
Spotted by: Paul Silom

→ TONGUE THAI'D
Location: Thailand
Spotted by: Richard Jones

The Sea

SPECIAL FOOD TODAY...

- TOMYAM KUNG   180 ฿
- TOM KAH GAI   120 ฿
- SPICY SEAFOOD SALAD 120B
- STIR FRIED CHICKEN WITH
  CASHEWNUTS   150 ฿
- PORK CHOP   250 ฿
- SIRLION STEAK   250 ฿
- FISH & CHIP   150 ฿

☆ THE SEA ☆

DARICHT BEER   60 ฿
HEINEKEN BEER   65 ฿
SINGHA BEER   65 ฿
CHANG BEER   60 ฿

                  120 ฿

COCKTAILS

- MARGARITA
- MAI-TAI
- BLUE HAWAII
- PENACOLADA
- PATTAWIA COOLER

THANK YOU ...

DARUGHT
BEER
60.-

Angry Potato

→ FIREY TEMPER
Location: Burma
Spotted by: David Sim

← BALLS UP
Location: Indonesia
Spotted by: Chris Reece

The Car dose not smell putrid

Big Taxi 7 seat

← TAXI RANK
Location: Thailand
Spotted by: Roland Banks

→ HAND ME THE BUCKET
Location: Thailand
Spotted by: Graeme Hamilton

KICKAPOO
Joy Juice
®

DAPATKAN KICK!

Net Volume: 1.5 L

S: AIR BERKARBONAT / CARBONATED WATER,
RIK / CITRIC ACID, NATRIUM BENZOAT / SODIUM
D EKSTRAK STEVIA / STEVIA EXTRACT.
DISIONER MAKANAN, BAHAN PERISA,
DAN PEWARNA YANG DIBENARKAN

↗ CRAP COMPARISON
Location: Malaysia
Spotted by: Howard Chapman

↙ PUT YOUR FOOT IN IT
Location: Malaysia
Spotted by: Marian Winterton

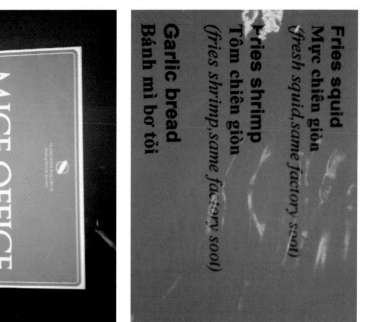

Fries squid
Mực chiên giòn
(fresh squid,same factory soot)

Fries shrimp
Tôm chiên giòn
(fries shrimp,same factory soot)

Garlic bread
Bánh mì bơ tỏi

← SAME OLD, SAME OLD
Location: Vietnam
Spotted by: Graham Law

← HOTEL FOR RODENTS
Location: Indonesia
Spotted by: Michael Black

→ DEFINE 'HAPPY'?
Location: Burma
Spotted by: Tim Campbell

→ ONLY THE FRESHEST INGREDIENTS

Location: Thailand
Spotted by: Ken Marsh

← GOT THE PAINTERS IN

Location: Thailand
Spotted by: Ian Gloag

↑ LET'S SEE THOSE TEETH!

Location: Vietnam
Spotted by: Chris Howling

↑ MARKETING GURU REQUIRED

Location: Thailand
Spotted by: Antranik K

→ CARRY ON IN THE MINIBUS

Location: Thailand
Spotted by: Jenny Barnett

↑ **HARD TO STOMACH**
Location: Thailand
Spotted by: Polly Mansell

← **SOMETHING FISHY**
Location: Thailand
Spotted by: Jim Cameron

← CHEEKY MONKEY
Location: Thailand
Spotted by: Pennie Uygurer

← PANNED DESIGNS
Location: Singapore
Spotted by: Brian Robinson

→ I'LL HAVE A BOWELFUL
Location: Thailand
Spotted by: Gerhard van Lochem

ปลาแชะบางาดดวาดหน้าร้านสาธรสด

DEEP FRIED SEA-BASS WITH CHILI SAUCE

ปลากะดีกย่าง   100

GRILLED SQUID

ปลาสำลิเผา (ราคาตามน้ำหนัก)   300-350

GRILLED SAMILTI FISH (Prices based on weight.)

ปลากะพงเผา   (ราคาตามน้ำหนัก)   300-350

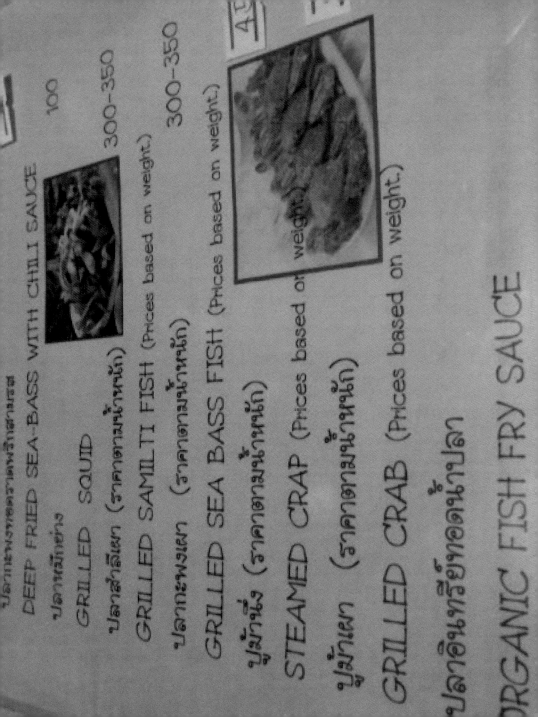

GRILLED SEA BASS FISH (Prices based on weight.)

ปูม้านึ่ง (ราคาตามน้ำหนัก)

STEAMED CRAP (Prices based on weight.)

ปูม้าเผา (ราคาตามน้ำหนัก)

GRILLED CRAB (Prices based on weight.)

ปลาอื่นหรือยำออแกานิค

ORGANIC FISH FRY SAUCE

→ AN INTIMATE RECEPTION
Location: Indonesia
Spotted by: Chris Reece

← RELAXED ATMOSPHERE
Location: Vietnam
Spotted by: Philip R. Slocum

← THE SIGN OF A GENTLEMAN
Location: Burma
Spotted by: Sue Gore

← RAISES A GOOD POINT
Location: Vietnam
Spotted by: Pauline Naylor

→ FORMAL BATHROOM
Location: Cambodia
Spotted by: Joanne Grant

SATISFACTORY FOOD RESTAURANT

TEL: 012 76 49 69 / 088 98 95 938

↑ WHERE THE SERVICE IS ACCEPTABLE
Location: Cambodia
Spotted by: Polly Mansell

← PATENT NONSENSE
Location: Laos
Spotted by: Laurence Ranson

AUSTRALASIA

Signs are guaranteed to make your head spin as soon as you arrive Down Under, and pick up your hire car. What do you do when faced with genuine towns like Wollomooloo and Wagga Wagga? Boing Boing or Humpty Doo? On New Zealand's North Island, you could even find yourself bound for the world's longest known place name (deep breath now: Taumata whaka tangi hanga koauau o tamatea turi pukakapi ki maunga horo nuku poka i whenua kitana tahu – or Taumata to the locals). Yes, things operate very differently

on the other side of the world, where women glow and men plunder (or so says Men at Work). It's the home of the largest living thing on earth (the Great Barrier Reef), the world's largest monolith (Uluru), the curious kiwi, the bizarre platypus, the haka…… oh, and more deadly creepy crawly things than you can shake a stick at. Although shaking a stick at any of the world's ten most poisonous snakes is generally not advised. Given all that, is it any wonder that their signs are a little eccentric?

DOGS
ARE NOT
PERMITTED
IN THE FLEA
MARKET
BY ORDER:
ENVIRONMENTAL HEALTH
OFFICER: Palmerston North City
Council

→ **DOWN CHUNDER**
Location: Australia
Spotted by: Kate Alley

→ **SOUND ADVICE**
Location: Australia
Spotted by: Elaine Norton

← **FUN IN THE SUN**
Location: Australia
Spotted by: Husam Fakhry

← WOMB WITH A VIEW
Location: Australia
Spotted by: Ruaridh Watson

RESTAURANT

**RE-OPEN
SOON**

Wife is on Break
aka BEEN SLACK 28/02/2013

← MATILDA WENT A WALTZING
Location: Tasmania
Spotted by: Gareth Powell

→ VEHICULAR VASECTOMY
Location: Australia
Spotted by: John Lawrenson

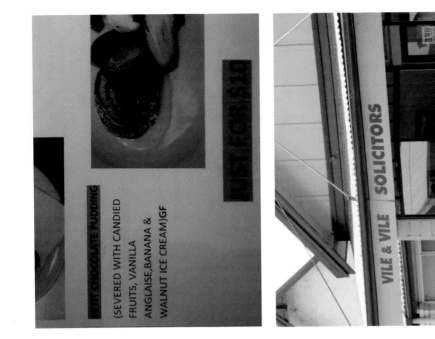

→ A CUT ABOVE
Location: New Zealand
Spotted by: Charlotte Vezine

→ BORN TO PRACTISE LAW
Location: Australia
Spotted by: Ken Harvey

← EATING AD NAUSEAM
Location: New Zealand
Spotted by: Richard Johnson

OPERATING HOURS

DAYLIGHT SAVING 9am–7pm
NON–D/LIGHT SAVING 9am–5pm

HOW TO GET ON BARGE

1. Drive up and down Car Park looking for Bridge.

2. Park at Information Centre.

3. Then park in Car Park.

4. Drive to Kiosk and ask is Barge Operator still in Bed, or how do you get across on Barge if there is no Operator?

5. The Quickest and Easiest way is when you are ready, Park on road at STOP SIGN and Operator will come.

← SORRY TO BARGE IN
Location: Tasmania
Spotted by: Jeff Tonge

→ EYE OFF THE BALL
Location: Australia
Spotted by: Andrew Bacon

→ AUSSIE RULES
Location: Australia
Spotted by: George Topfner

WARNING

DO NOT READ THIS SIGN